W0090485

PASSIONS...

Beaches

PASSIONS...

Beaches

PHOTOGRAPHS SUPPLIED BY AXIOM PHOTOGRAPHIC AGENCY

DREAM PLACES YOU'D RATHER BE

DUNCAN BAIRD PUBLISHERS
LONDON

PASSIONS... *Beaches*

First published in the United Kingdom and
Ireland in 2005 by
Duncan Baird Publishers Ltd
Sixth Floor
Castle House
75–76 Wells Street
London W1T 3QH

Conceived, created and designed by
Duncan Baird Publishers

Managing Editor: Kirsten Chapman
Managing Designer: Manisha Patel
Picture Researcher: Louise Glasson

British Library Cataloguing-in-Publication Data:
A CIP record for this book is available from the
British Library

ISBN-10: 1-84483-162-0
ISBN-13: 9-781844-831623

10 9 8 7 6 5 4 3 2 1

Typeset in Bergell and Futura
Colour reproduction by Colourscan, Singapore
Printed in Singapore by Imago

Foreword

AS THE SUN RISES, WAVES BREAK LANGUIDLY ON
THE SHORE, EASY IN THEIR AGE-OLD RHYTHM. EARLY
MORNING IS A MAGICAL TIME ON THE BEACH.
THERE'S PEACE IN THE SOLITUDE. THE COOL BREEZE
AND CLEAR WATERS WASH THE SLEEP FROM YOUR
BODY. AND THE DAY IS FULL OF PROMISE.

GRADUALLY THE SUN GLIDES HIGHER IN THE
SKY, INTENSIFYING THE COLOURS OF THE SCENE –
THE RICH, SUCCULENT GREEN OF THE COCONUT
PALMS; A SUBLIME WHITE CRESCENT OF SAND; AND
ENDLESS AZURE WATERS, SPRINKLED WITH DROPS OF

SUNLIGHT AND SOFT, WHITE FOAM. THE SUN ALSO RADIATES A DELICIOUS WARMTH, WHICH SEEPS INTO YOUR SKIN AND DEEP INTO YOUR MUSCLES, RELEASING TENSIONS AND INVIGORATING EVERY PART OF YOUR BODY.

EVERYTHING SLOWS TO THE PACE OF NATURE. THE DAY IS FILLED WITH THE SIMPLEST OF PLEASURES: SWINGING GENTLY IN A HAMMOCK; STROLLING THROUGH THE SHALLOWS; SPYING ON THE ANTICS OF BRIGHTLY SHINING FISH; DISCOVERING SECLUDED HIDEAWAYS AMONG THE ROCKS AND SAND DUNES.

THE HOURS DRIFT BY LAZILY AND HAPPILY, UNTIL THE SUN STARTS SINKING TOWARD THE WESTERN HORIZON, SIGNALLING THE BEGINNING OF THE SPECTACULAR EVENING DISPLAY – A SLOW-MOVING GLORY OF ORANGES, PINKS, REDS AND PURPLES.

WHEREVER YOU ARE IN THE WORLD, ALL THE SENSATIONS OF THE BEACH COMBINE PERFECTLY TO INSPIRE YOU AND LEAVE YOU WITH A PROFOUND SENSE OF WELL-BEING. THE BEACH IS A PLACE TO ENJOY YOUR OWN COMPANY OR SHARE TIME WITH

FRIENDS. WHAT'S MORE, IT'S A PLACE IN WHICH YOU CAN THINK AND DREAM. WE HOPE YOU FIND ALL THIS AND MORE IN THE PAGES OF THIS BOOK ...

"Twenty years from now you will be more disappointed by the things you didn't do than by the ones you did .... Sail away .... Explore. Dream. Discover."

MARK TWAIN (1835-1910)

"The good and the wise
lead quiet lives."

EURIPIDES (C.485–C.406 BC)

"The world is a book,
and those who do not
travel read only a page."

SAINT AUGUSTINE (354–430)

"My first idea of the movement of the dance certainly came from the rhythm of the waves."

ISADORA DUNCAN (1878–1927)

"Simplicity is the ultimate sophistication."

LEONARDO DA VINCI (1452–1519)

"Touch the earth, love the
earth, honor the earth,
her plains, her valleys,
her hills and her seas;
rest your spirit in her
solitary places."

HENRY BESTON (1888–1968)

"Walk barefoot on distant sands, amid the brightly painted boats at rest."

CONNOR READE (1932–99)

49

"Sand, sea and sky —
a progression toward the
sublime. Inwardly,
unconsciously, we complete
the series: heaven."

LOUISE SOUSTELLE (1911–62)

"Sit in reverie, and watch the changing color of the waves that break upon the idle seashore of the mind."

HENRY WADSWORTH LONGFELLOW (1807–82)

"You must live in the
present, launch yourself
on every wave, find your
eternity in each moment."

HENRY DAVID THOREAU (1817–62)

"The cure for anything
is salt water — sweat,
tears or the sea."

ISAK DINESEN (1865–1962)

"There is a rapture on the
lonely shore,
There is society where none
intrudes
By the deep sea, and music
in its roar."

LORD BYRON (1788–1824)

"To do nothing at all is the most difficult thing in the world, the most difficult and the most intellectual."

OSCAR WILDE (1854–1900)

"A happy life consists in tranquillity of mind."

CICERO (106–43 BC)

"If the sight of the blue skies fills you with joy .... if the simple things of nature have a message that you understand, rejoice, for your soul is alive ...."

ELEONORA DUSE (1859–1924)

"Summer isles of Eden,
lying in dark purple
spheres of sea."

LORD ALFRED TENNYSON (1809–92)

"The world is round and the place which may seem like the end may also be only the beginning."

IVY BAKER PRIEST (1905–75)

Locations

Text credits

Picture credits

All photographs by Axiom Photographic Agency, London.